CLEARWATER
TRAVEL GUIDE

Discover Clearwater: Maps, Directions, Culture, Top Attractions, Accommodations, Airports, Banks, Restaurants, Festivals, Culinary, Itinerary, Nightlife & others

JOHN P. WADE

DISCLAIMER

ABOUT THE AUTHOR

John P. Wade, a native of the United States and a resident of North America, is a dedicated travel guide author with a passion for exploring the world's wonders. With a loving family by his side, he navigates the globe, immersing himself in diverse cultures and sharing his travel expertise to promote the joy of travel and tourism.

Married and a proud parent, John understands the importance of family adventures and brings this perspective into his travel guides. His insights resonate with fellow travelers, offering a unique blend of practical advice and heartfelt experiences.

In addition to his role as a travel guide, John is a voracious reader, finding inspiration in the pages of books from around the world. He channels his creativity into making music, capturing the essence of his journeys through melodies that resonate with the soul. His love for laughter is evident in his talent for crafting jokes, adding a touch of humor to his interactions and writings.

For travel enthusiasts seeking more than just destinations, John P. Wade offers a holistic approach to exploration. Through his travel guides, he not only guides you to picturesque locations but also invites you to experience the joy of travel with your loved ones. Embark on a journey of discovery and laughter with John, where every adventure becomes a cherished memory.

TABLE OF CONTENT

INTRODUCTION

Destination Overview

Brief History

Nestled along Florida's Gulf Coast, Clearwater's history is as vibrant as its sunsets. Long before the sandy beaches became a tourist haven, indigenous Tocobaga and Calusa tribes called this region home. Their presence laid the groundwork for what would later become a fascinating blend of heritage and modernity.

Early Settlements and Agriculture
Spanish explorers arrived in the 16th century, leaving their mark on the area. However, it wasn't until the mid-1800s that Clearwater

witnessed significant settlement. Pioneers, attracted by the fertile land, established farming communities. Citrus groves and vegetable farms flourished, shaping the landscape and economy.

Arrival of the Railroad

The early 20th century marked a pivotal moment with the arrival of the railroad. This development catapulted Clearwater into a new era, opening doors for trade and tourism. The pristine beaches and warm climate attracted visitors seeking an escape from the bustling cities.

Rise of Tourism

As the 1920s unfolded, Clearwater's reputation as a tourist destination solidified. Hotels, including the landmark Belleview Biltmore, welcomed guests eager to experience the coastal paradise. The influx of visitors brought prosperity, and Clearwater's identity began to intertwine with its role as a leisure destination.

Development and Modernization

Post-World War II, Clearwater experienced rapid growth and modernization. The construction of the Clearwater Memorial Causeway in the 1960s improved accessibility, further boosting tourism. The city embraced its waterfront location, fostering a lifestyle centered around the sea.

Challenges and Resilience

Clearwater, like any community, faced challenges. Hurricanes, economic shifts, and environmental concerns tested its resilience. However, the city has consistently bounced back, demonstrating a determination to preserve its natural beauty and cultural heritage.

Today's Clearwater

Modern Clearwater is a dynamic blend of its storied past and contemporary allure. Visitors can explore historic neighborhoods, indulge in diverse culinary experiences, and bask in the beauty of its beaches. The city continues to evolve, welcoming new generations while honoring the traditions that make Clearwater a timeless destination.

As you embark on your Clearwater adventure, take a moment to appreciate the layers of history that have shaped this coastal gem. From Native American roots to the bustling tourist destination it is today, Clearwater's journey is etched in the very fabric of its sun-soaked shores.

Geography and Climate

Geography

Situated on the west coast of Florida, Clearwater enjoys a prime location surrounded by natural beauty. The city is part of Pinellas County, known for its picturesque landscapes and waterfront charm. Clearwater Beach, a barrier island, is a highlight, offering pristine shores and panoramic views of the Gulf of Mexico.

Intracoastal Waterway: Clearwater is graced by the Intracoastal Waterway, providing scenic water views and opportunities for boating and water sports.

Beaches: Beyond the renowned Clearwater Beach, explore nearby gems like Sand Key Park for a quieter coastal experience.

Climate

Clearwater boasts a subtropical climate, ensuring a sun-soaked experience for most of the year.

Summers: Warm and humid, with temperatures ranging from the mid-70s to the high 80s Fahrenheit. Expect occasional afternoon showers, refreshing the atmosphere.

Winters: Mild and pleasant, with temperatures averaging in the 60s and 70s Fahrenheit. Winter is the peak tourist season, drawing visitors escaping colder climates.

Hurricane Season: June to November marks the hurricane season. While direct hits are rare, it's advisable to stay informed and prepared.

Clearwater's geography and climate create an inviting backdrop for a range of activities, making it a year-round destination for those seeking sun, sea, and a touch of adventure.

CHAPTER ONE

Maps and Directions

Clearwater Maps:
https://maps.app.goo.gl/MEgYXLf9BKPEh3cT7

Detailed Maps and Key Areas

City Layout
Clearwater's well-organized layout facilitates easy exploration, with distinct areas catering to various interests.

1. Downtown Clearwater: The heart of the city, offering a mix of historic charm and modern amenities. Explore Cleveland Street for shopping, dining, and cultural experiences.

2. Clearwater Beach: A barrier island paradise with a lively atmosphere. The Beach Walk promenade connects various attractions, from Pier 60 to beachside restaurants and shops.

3. *Island Estates:* Connected to Clearwater Beach by the Memorial Causeway, this residential area provides a more relaxed ambiance while being close to the action.

4. *North Clearwater:* Home to parks like Moccasin Lake Nature Park and Countryside Recreation Center, providing green spaces and recreational facilities.

Detailed Maps

1. Downtown Clearwater Map:
- Highlights key landmarks like Coachman Park and the Clearwater Main Library.

- Indicates parking areas for convenient access to downtown attractions.

- Pinpoints popular dining spots, from local eateries to fine dining.

2. Clearwater Beach Map:

- Details the layout of Clearwater Beach, highlighting public beach access points.

- Indicates the location of beach amenities, including showers, restrooms, and picnic areas.

- Identifies beachfront hotels, allowing visitors to choose accommodations with proximity to the shoreline.

3. *Island Estates Map:*
- Illustrates the residential layout of Island Estates.

- Highlights the Memorial Causeway connecting the island to Clearwater Beach.

- Notes points of interest, such as local markets and parks.

Key Areas of Interest

1. Pier 60:

- An iconic spot for sunset celebrations with daily festivities, street performers, and a vibrant atmosphere.

- Fishing opportunities from the pier.

- Nearby shops and restaurants.

2. Clearwater Marine Aquarium:

- Home to Winter the Dolphin, known for its prosthetic tail and featured in movies.

- Educational exhibits on marine life conservation.

- Opportunities for interactive experiences.

3. Sand Key Park:

- A quieter alternative to Clearwater Beach, known for its natural beauty.

- Offers picnic areas, walking trails, and beach access.

- Perfect for a serene beach day.

Insider Tips

Useful Apps: Utilize navigation apps for real-time directions and traffic updates.

Biking and Walking Trails: Discover Clearwater's beauty by exploring the various biking and walking trails, especially along the Beach Walk.

Explore Beyond the Beach: While Clearwater Beach is a highlight, venture into neighborhoods like downtown and Island Estates for a well-rounded experience.

Clearwater's detailed maps and key areas guide you through a city rich in diversity, ensuring you make the most of your visit by discovering both popular attractions and hidden gems.

Travel Resources and Websites

Make the most of your experience with these travel resources and websites that provide valuable information and assistance.

1. Clearwater Official Tourism Website:
https://www.visitclearwaterflorida.com/

The official tourism website is a comprehensive guide offering details on attractions, events, accommodations, and more. Stay updated on current promotions and local happenings.

2. City of Clearwater Official Website:
https://www.myclearwater.com/

For practical information on local services, city events, and community news, the official city website is a go-to resource. Explore city services, parks, and community programs.

3. Clearwater Beach Chamber of Commerce:

Website: https://www.beachchamber.com/

The Chamber of Commerce website provides insights into local businesses, events, and services. Access a business directory and discover exclusive offers from Clearwater Beach establishments.

4. Transportation Resources:

PSTA (Pinellas Suncoast Transit Authority):
- [RidePSTA.net] or https://www.ridepsta.net/

- Clearwater Ferry: [ClearwaterFerry.com] or https://www.clearwaterferry.com/

Utilize PSTA for public transportation information and routes, while the Clearwater Ferry offers scenic water transportation between Clearwater Beach and downtown.

5. Weather Updates:

- National Weather Service: https://www.weather.gov/

Stay informed about Clearwater's weather conditions, especially if you plan outdoor activities. The National Weather Service provides accurate and up-to-date forecasts.

6. Interactive Maps:

Google Maps:
https://www.google.com/maps

Navigate Clearwater effortlessly with Google Maps, which offers real-time directions, traffic updates, and details on nearby attractions.

7. Local Events Calendar:

Clearwater Events Calendar: https://www.clearwaterevents.com/

Discover upcoming events, festivals, and activities in Clearwater. Plan your visit around local celebrations for an immersive experience.

8. Hotel and Accommodation Booking:
https://www.booking.com/

Find and compare hotel options in Clearwater using Booking.com. Filter results based on preferences and read reviews from fellow travelers.

9. Flight Information:

St. Pete-Clearwater International Airport:
https://fly2pie.com/

For those flying in, check the official airport website for flight information, services, and transportation options.

10. Social Media:

Follow Clearwater's tourism boards, local businesses, and influencers on platforms like Instagram, Twitter, and Facebook for real-time updates, travel tips, and inspiring visuals.

With these resources at your fingertips, your Clearwater journey is bound to be smooth and memorable.

Recommended Tour Operators

Embarking on a Clearwater adventure is a seamless experience when guided by skilled tour operators. These professionals elevate your journey, providing insights, access to hidden gems, and curated experiences. Here are some recommended tour operators to enhance your exploration of Clearwater:

1. Little Toot Dolphin Adventures:

Website:https://www.littletoot.us/

Board the iconic Little Toot, a spirited tugboat, for a dolphin-watching experience like no other. The knowledgeable crew ensures a front-row seat to playful dolphins dancing in the wake, creating memories that linger long after the tour.

2. Encounters With Dolphins:

Website: https://encounterswithdolphins.com/

Specializing in intimate dolphin encounters, this operator offers guided boat tours that prioritize responsible wildlife viewing. Navigate the Gulf's crystalline waters and witness these majestic creatures in their natural habitat.

3. Pirate Rides Clearwater:
Website: https://pirateridesofclearwater.com/

For a family-friendly adventure, set sail with Pirate Rides Clearwater. This swashbuckling experience combines entertainment and education, making it an ideal choice for those traveling with children.

4. Clearwater Beach WaveRunner Rentals:
Website: https://www.cbjetski.com/

For thrill-seekers, Clearwater Beach WaveRunner Rentals provides high-speed jet ski adventures. Explore the coastline, feel the wind in your hair, and add an adrenaline kick to your Clearwater escapade.

5. Tampa Bay Escape Room:

Website: [TampaBayEscapeRoom.com] or Click here

Immerse yourself in an interactive experience with Tampa Bay Escape Room, offering themed challenges that stimulate the mind. Perfect for groups, this operator adds a unique dimension to your Clearwater visit.

6. Dolphin Paradise Tours:

Website: [DolphinParadiseTours.com] or Click here

Embark on a private tour with Dolphin Paradise Tours for a personalized encounter with Clearwater's marine life. The knowledgeable guides cater to your preferences, ensuring a tailored and memorable experience.

7. Cycle Brewing Tours:

Website: [CycleBrewingTours.com] or Click here

Explore Clearwater's burgeoning craft beer scene with Cycle Brewing Tours. Hop between local breweries, savoring unique brews while gaining insights into the city's craft beer culture.

8. Sea Screamer Clearwater:

Website: [SeaScreamer.com] or Click here

For a thrilling adventure on the high seas, join Sea Screamer Clearwater, the world's largest speedboat. Feel the wind rush as you cruise the

Gulf, spotting dolphins and enjoying the exhilarating ride.

Tips for Choosing a Tour Operator:

Reviews and Ratings: Check online reviews to gauge the experiences of fellow travelers.

Safety Measures: Prioritize operators with clear safety protocols for a worry-free experience.

Tour Duration and Inclusions: Assess the duration of the tour and what is included to ensure it aligns with your preferences.

With these recommended tour operators, your Clearwater exploration promises to be not only memorable but also expertly guided, ensuring you make the most of this coastal paradise.

Important Phone Numbers and Contacts for a Seamless Clearwater Experience

When navigating the enchanting world of Clearwater, having access to important phone numbers and contacts ensures a smooth and enjoyable journey. Whether you need assistance, information, or emergency services, these essential contacts are your go-to resources:

1. Emergency Services:

Police, Fire, Medical Emergency: 911

In case of any emergencies, dial **911** for immediate assistance. Clearwater's emergency services are responsive and equipped to handle a range of situations.

2. City Services and Information:

- City of Clearwater General Inquiries: **727-562-4040**

- Clearwater Parks & Recreation: **727-562-4800**

For non-emergency city-related queries, including information about parks, recreation facilities, and local services, these numbers provide valuable assistance.

3. Clearwater Visitor Information Center:

- Visitor Information Hotline: **727-464-7200**

Connect with the Clearwater Visitor Information Center for details about attractions, events, and general travel information.

4. Clearwater Marine Aquarium:

- Main Line: **727-441-1790**

- Dolphin Tale Hotline:**727-441-4141**

For inquiries about exhibits, educational programs, and encounters with marine life, the Clearwater Marine Aquarium contacts are invaluable.

5. St. Pete-Clearwater International Airport:

Main Line: **727-453-7800**

If you are flying in or out of Clearwater, the airport's main line provides information about flights, services, and transportation options.

6. Public Transportation:

- PSTA (Pinellas Suncoast Transit Authority): **727-540-1900**
- Clearwater Ferry: **727-755-0297**

For public transportation information and details about ferry services, these contacts will assist you in navigating Clearwater efficiently.

7. Hospital and Medical Services:

- Morton Plant Hospital: **727-462-7000**

In the event of medical emergencies or healthcare needs, Morton Plant Hospital is a trusted healthcare facility in Clearwater.

8. Weather Updates:

- National Weather Service: **727-539-6421**

Stay informed about Clearwater's weather conditions by contacting the National Weather Service for accurate and up-to-date forecasts.

9. Clearwater Beach Chamber of Commerce:

- Chamber Information: **727-447-7600**

For business-related inquiries, local events, and recommendations, the Clearwater Beach Chamber of Commerce is a valuable resource.

10. Lost and Found (City of Clearwater):

- City of Clearwater Lost and Found: **727-562-4040**

If you misplace items or have lost something during your visit, contact the City of Clearwater's Lost and Found for assistance.

Tips for Utilizing Contacts:

Save Numbers: Save essential numbers in your phone for quick access.

Emergency Protocol: Familiarize yourself with emergency protocols and locations of nearby services.

With these important phone numbers and contacts at your fingertips, your Clearwater adventure is not only exciting but also backed by the support and information needed for a memorable experience.

CHAPTER TWO

Planning Your Trips

Best Time to Visit Clearwater

Clearwater's allure is ever-present, but the ideal time to visit depends on your preferences and the experiences you seek. Consider these seasonal nuances when planning your Clearwater getaway:

1. Peak Season: Winter (December - February)

Weather: Mild temperatures ranging from the 60s to 70s Fahrenheit.

Attractions: Ideal for beach lovers and outdoor activities.

Events: Clearwater enjoys a lively atmosphere with festivals and events.

Crowds: Popular tourist season, so expect larger crowds and higher accommodation rates.

2. Shoulder Seasons: Fall (September - November) and Spring (March - May)

Weather: Pleasant temperatures, ranging from the 70s to 80s Fahrenheit.

Attractions: Enjoy outdoor activities without the peak-season crowds.

Events: Fall brings fewer events, while spring witnesses a resurgence of festivals.

Affordability: Accommodation rates may be more budget-friendly compared to peak season.

3. Summer (June - August)

Weather: Warm temperatures, often in the high 80s to low 90s Fahrenheit.

Attractions: Perfect for water sports and beach activities.

Events: Summer events and festivals add vibrancy.

Crowds: Popular among families and students on vacation, leading to increased crowds.

4. Hurricane Season (June - November)

Considerations: Be aware of the hurricane season, with increased rain and the possibility of storms.

Advantages: Lower accommodation rates and fewer crowds if you're willing to navigate occasional rain showers.

Tips for Choosing the Best Time:

1. *Personal Preferences:* Determine whether you prefer vibrant crowds, quieter escapes, or specific weather conditions.

2. *Budget Considerations:* Accommodation rates vary by season, so plan accordingly based on your budget.

3. *Events and Festivals*: Check the events calendar if you want to coincide your visit with festivals or special activities.

4. *Outdoor Activities:* Consider the activities you have in mind, whether it's beach days, water sports, or exploring nature trails.

5. *Weather Tolerance:* Be mindful of your tolerance for heat, as summers can be warm, while winters are milder.

Clearwater, with its year-round sunshine, offers something for every traveler. Whether you seek the lively energy of peak season or the quieter charm of shoulder seasons, your Clearwater experience awaits.

Travel Budgeting

Embarking on a Clearwater adventure involves strategic budgeting to ensure a seamless and enjoyable experience. From accommodation to activities and dining, consider these factors to make the most of your budget while exploring this coastal paradise:

1. Accommodation:

Range of Options: Clearwater offers a variety of accommodation options, from luxury beachfront resorts to budget-friendly motels.

Booking in Advance: Secure your stay by booking accommodation in advance, especially during peak seasons, to avail of early-bird discounts.

Alternative Stays: Explore vacation rentals or boutique hotels for unique experiences that might align with your budget.

2. Transportation:

Airport Transportation: Compare prices for airport transfers or consider public transportation options like shuttle services for cost-effective travel.

Car Rentals: If planning to explore beyond Clearwater, consider renting a car for flexibility. Compare prices and book in advance for potential discounts.

Public Transportation: Utilize the Pinellas Suncoast Transit Authority (PSTA) buses for an affordable means of getting around the city.

3. Dining:

Local Eateries: Explore local restaurants and eateries for authentic flavors and often more budget-friendly options than tourist-centric spots.

Grocery Stores: Consider occasional meals from grocery stores or farmers' markets for cost-effective dining.

Happy Hour Deals: Take advantage of happy hour specials at beachside bars and restaurants for discounted drinks and appetizers.

4. Activities and Attractions:

Package Deals: Check for bundled tickets or packages for popular attractions to save on individual entry fees.

Free Activities: Enjoy the natural beauty of Clearwater's beaches and parks, which often come with no admission fees.

Local Discounts: Look for local discounts or city passes that provide access to multiple attractions at a reduced cost.

5. Shopping:

Local Markets: Explore local markets for unique souvenirs and gifts, often at more affordable prices than tourist shops.

Outlet Shopping: Clearwater is near outlet malls, offering brand-name items at discounted prices.

6. Tips for Budgeting:

Research and Plan: Research prices and plan your itinerary to allocate your budget effectively.

Set Daily Limits: Establish daily spending limits to manage your expenses throughout the trip.

Off-Peak Travel: Consider traveling during the shoulder seasons or off-peak times for potential cost savings.

Cash vs. Card: While cards are convenient, having some cash on hand is useful for small purchases and places that may not accept cards.

Emergency Fund: Include a buffer in your budget for unexpected expenses or spontaneous activities.

Clearwater's beauty and experiences can be enjoyed on various budgets. By strategically planning and making informed choices, you can create a memorable journey without breaking the bank. Whether you're a budget-conscious traveler or looking for a luxurious experience, Clearwater welcomes you to explore its treasures at your own pace.

Visa and Entry Requirements for Clearwater

Before embarking on your journey to Clearwater, it's crucial to understand the visa and entry requirements to ensure a seamless and hassle-free experience. Here's a comprehensive guide to help you navigate the entry process:

1. Visa Requirements:

Visa-Free Travel: Travelers from many countries, including those from the Visa Waiver Program (VWP), can enter the United States for short visits without a visa.

Visa for Extended Stays: If planning an extended stay or for purposes other than tourism, a visa may be required. Check with the nearest U.S. embassy or consulate for specific details.

Electronic System for Travel Authorization (ESTA): Travelers under the VWP must apply for ESTA approval online before boarding their flight.

2. Passport Requirements:

Valid Passport: Ensure your passport is valid for at least six months beyond your intended departure date from the United States.

Blank Visa Pages: Check if your passport has enough blank pages for entry stamps.

3. Travel Authorization for Certain Countries:

Check Requirements: Citizens of certain countries may require additional travel authorizations or visas. Specific requirements should be confirmed based on your nationality.

4. Arrival in Clearwater:

Airport Immigration: Clearwater does not have its own international airport. The nearest major airport is Tampa International Airport (TPA), where you will go through U.S. immigration and customs.

Customs Declaration: Complete a customs declaration form, declaring any items you are bringing into the country.

5. Health and Vaccination Requirements:

No Specific Vaccinations: There are no specific vaccinations required for entry into Clearwater. It's advisable however, to be up-to-date on vaccines routine.

6. Currency Declaration:

Currency Limits: If carrying more than **$10,000** in currency, it must be declared upon entry.

7. Transportation to Clearwater:

Domestic Flights: If arriving from another U.S. city, there are no immigration procedures, but security checks are standard.

International Flights: For international flights, follow the procedures at the first U.S. port of entry.

8. Extension of Stay:

Visa Extensions: If you need to extend your stay, apply for an extension well in advance of your authorized period of stay expiration.

9. Tips for Smooth Entry:

Documentation: Carry printed copies of your travel authorizations, hotel reservations, and return flight details.

Communication: Be prepared to answer questions from immigration officers truthfully and concisely.

Know Your Itinerary: Familiarize yourself with your travel itinerary, accommodation details, and planned activities.

By understanding and adhering to these entry requirements, you set the stage for a stress-free and enjoyable stay in Clearwater. Stay informed, plan ahead, and embark on your journey to this coastal paradise with confidence.

Health and Safety Tips:

Ensuring your well-being is paramount when exploring Clearwater's beauty. Consider these health and safety tips to make the most of your journey while prioritizing your health:

1. Sun Protection:

Sunscreen: Florida's sun is potent. Pack and regularly apply a broad-spectrum sunscreen with at least SPF 30.

Protective Gear: Wear a wide-brimmed hat, sunglasses, and lightweight, long-sleeved clothing for added protection.

2. Hydration:

Water Intake: Stay hydrated, especially in the warm months. Drink (water) regularly and always go along with a reusable water bottle.

Avoid Dehydration: Limit alcohol consumption, as it can contribute to dehydration.

3. Insect Protection:

Repellent: Apply insect repellent, especially if venturing into wooded areas or during dusk and dawn.

Protective Clothing: Wear long sleeves and pants in areas with dense vegetation.

4. Health Precautions:

Vaccinations: Ensure routine vaccinations are up to date. For any recommended vaccinations, check your healthcare provider.

Travel Insurance: Consider travel insurance that covers medical emergencies and unexpected events.

5. COVID-19 Considerations:

Check Guidelines: Stay informed about COVID-19 guidelines and restrictions. Check for any specific requirements for your travel dates.

Mask Usage: Be aware of mask policies in public spaces and adhere to them.

6. Water Safety:

Swimming Vigilance: If swimming in the Gulf of Mexico, be mindful of strong currents. Heed warnings and lifeguard instructions.

Water Activities: Follow safety instructions for water activities and sports. Use life jackets when appropriate.

7. Food and Water Safety:

Safe Dining Practices: Choose restaurants with good hygiene practices. Ensure food is thoroughly cooked, and avoid street vendors if uncertain about food safety.

Bottled Water: If concerned about tap water, opt for bottled water to stay hydrated.

8. Heat Awareness:

Midday Breaks: Plan outdoor activities in the morning or late afternoon to avoid peak heat hours.

Heatstroke Prevention: Recognize signs of heat-related illnesses and take breaks in shaded areas.

9. Crime Awareness:

Safe Areas: Clearwater is generally safe, but like any destination, be aware of your surroundings. Always be in well-lit and populated areas.

Secure Belongings: Keep valuables secure and be cautious in crowded areas.

10. Local Healthcare:

Know Locations: Familiarize yourself with the locations of nearby pharmacies, urgent care centers, and hospitals.

Prescription Medications: Carry necessary medications and a copy of prescriptions.

11. Weather Awareness:

Hurricane Preparedness: If visiting during hurricane season (June to November), stay informed about weather updates and follow local advisories.

Lightning Safety: Be cautious during thunderstorms and seek shelter indoors.

12. Traveling with Medications:

Prescription Information: Carry a list of your prescription medications, including generic names.

Accessibility: Ensure you have enough medication for the duration of your stay and that it is easily accessible.

13. COVID-19 Testing:

Check Requirements: If your travel plans involve COVID-19 testing, be aware of testing requirements and locations.

Testing Facilities: Know the locations of testing facilities in Clearwater.

14. Local Guidelines and Resources:

Tourist Information Centers: Visit local information centers for additional safety tips and resources.

Local Authorities: Follow any guidelines or instructions provided by local authorities.

By prioritizing health and safety, you pave the way for a worry-free and enjoyable experience in Clearwater. Stay informed, be cautious, and savor every moment of this coastal paradise with peace of mind.

Packing List and Travel Gear

Prepare for your Clearwater adventure with a well-thought-out packing list and essential travel gear. Whether you're soaking up the sun on Clearwater Beach or exploring the city's vibrant neighborhoods, here's a comprehensive guide to ensure you have everything you need:

Clothing

Swimwear:
- Pack a couple of swimsuits for beach days or water activities.

Lightweight Clothing:
- Lightweight, breathable clothing for the warm Florida weather.

- Comfortable shorts, t-shirts, and sundresses.

Long Sleeves and Pants:
- Protect yourself from the sun with long-sleeved shirts and pants.

- Useful for evenings or if you plan on exploring wooded areas.

Comfortable Walking Shoes:
- Sandals for the beach and comfortable walking shoes for exploring the city.

Hat and Sunglasses:
- Shield from the sun using a wide-brimmed hat.

- Polarized sunglasses for added eye protection.

Light Jacket or Sweater:
- Evenings might get cooler, especially in the winter months.

Beach and Outdoor Essentials

Beach Towel:

- A lightweight, quick-drying towel for beach days.

Beach Bag:

- A spacious beach bag to carry essentials like sunscreen, water, and snacks.

Sunscreen:

- High SPF sunscreen to protect your skin from the strong Florida sun.

Reusable Water Bottle:

- Stay hydrated with a reusable water bottle.

Snorkeling Gear:

- If you plan on exploring marine life, consider bringing your snorkeling gear.

Electronics and Accessories

Camera or Smartphone:

- Capture the beauty of Clearwater with a camera or smartphone.

Portable Charger:
- Keep your devices charged while exploring.

Travel Adapter:
- An adapter to charge your electronic devices.

Health and Safety

First Aid Kit:
- Basic first aid supplies, including band-aids, pain relievers, and any necessary prescription medications.

Insect Repellent:
- Especially when exploring nature trails.

Personal Hygiene Items:
- Travel-sized toiletries, toothbrush, toothpaste, etc.

Documents and Essentials

Passport and ID:

- At least six months beyond your intended departure date, ensure your passport is valid.

Travel Insurance:

- Copy of your travel insurance policy.

Money and Cards:

- Sufficient cash and credit/debit cards.

Miscellaneous

Daypack or Backpack:

- For carrying essentials and day trips, use a small backpack.

Umbrella or Poncho:

- Florida weather can be unpredictable; be prepared for rain.

Travel Pillow:

- Especially if you have a long flight.

Guidebook or Map:

- A Clearwater travel guidebook or map for easy navigation.

COVID-19 Considerations

Face Masks:

- Carry multiple masks and follow any local guidelines.

Hand Sanitizer:

- Keep a small bottle of hand sanitizer for on-the-go cleanliness.

Tips for Packing

Roll Clothes: You save space and minimize wrinkles by rolling clothes.

Pack Essentials in Carry-On: Keep important documents, medications, and a change of clothes in your carry-on bag.

Check Airline Baggage Policies: Be aware of baggage weight limits and restrictions.

Leave Room for Souvenirs: If you plan on shopping, leave some space in your luggage for souvenirs.

With this comprehensive packing list, you'll be well-equipped for your Clearwater adventure. Tailor it to your specific needs and activities, and get ready to make the most of your time in this coastal paradise.

CHAPTER THREE

Flights, Airports, Transportation and Accommodations

Guide to Flights and Airports

Embark on your Clearwater journey with ease by understanding the flight options and airports that serve this coastal haven. Here's a comprehensive guide to help you navigate your arrival in Clearwater:

1. Tampa International Airport (TPA)

Address: 4100 George J. Bean Pkwy., Tampa, FL 33607
Phone Number: **813-870-8700**

Location: Tampa International Airport, located approximately 20 miles southeast of Clearwater, is the primary gateway to the region.

Airlines: TPA serves as a hub for multiple major airlines, offering a wide range of domestic and international flights.

Ground Transportation: Options include rental cars, shuttles, taxis, and rideshare services like Uber and Lyft.

Airport Facilities: TPA boasts a variety of services, including dining options, shopping, lounges, and amenities to make your arrival or departure comfortable.

Destination: 75 domestic and 20 international destinations

2. St. Pete-Clearwater International Airport (PIE):

Address: 14700 Terminal Blvd #221, Clearwater, FL 33762, United States

Phone Number: +1 727-453-7800

Location: Situated about 9 miles north of Clearwater's city center, PIE is a convenient airport option for travelers heading directly to Clearwater.

Airlines: PIE is served by several low-cost carriers and offers a range of domestic flights.

Ground Transportation: Ground transportation options include rental cars, taxis, and rideshare services. Shuttle services may also be available.

Airport Facilities: While smaller than TPA, PIE provides essential services, including dining options, car rental facilities, and other amenities for travelers.

Website: https://fly2pie.com/

3. Clearwater Airpark (CLW)
Address: 1000 N Hercules Ave, Clearwater, FL 33765, USA
Phone Number: 727 325-5957

Location: Clearwater Airpark is a general aviation airport primarily used for private and smaller aircraft.

Services: While it doesn't cater to commercial flights, Clearwater Airpark is essential for private and recreational aviators.

4. Choosing Your Arrival Airport:

TPA vs. PIE: Your choice between Tampa International Airport (TPA) and St. Pete-Clearwater International Airport (PIE) might depend on factors like *flight availability, airlines, and your proximity to each airport.*

Private Aviation: If arriving on a private or chartered flight, Clearwater Airpark may be a suitable option, offering convenience for smaller aircraft.

5. Booking Flights

Flight Options: Clearwater's proximity to Tampa provides numerous flight options. Utilize online platforms or consult travel agencies to find the best deals.

Flexible Dates: Be flexible with your travel dates to potentially secure more affordable flights.

Connecting Flights: Depending on your location, connecting flights might be necessary. Consider layover durations and airport facilities when choosing connecting flights.

6. Travel Tips

Arrival Planning: Consider your transportation options from the airport to your accommodation. Rental cars, shuttles, and rideshare services are readily available.

Arrive Early: Arrive at the airport well in advance, especially during peak travel times, to allow for security checks and any unexpected delays.

Baggage Policies: Be aware of baggage policies for your chosen airline to avoid surprises at check-in.

COVID-19 Considerations: Check and adhere to any travel restrictions, guidelines, or safety measures related to COVID-19. This includes mask requirements, testing protocols, and quarantine rules.

By understanding the flight options and features of each airport, you can tailor your arrival to suit your preferences and make the most of your introduction to Clearwater. Whether you land at the bustling Tampa International Airport or the conveniently located St. Pete-Clearwater International Airport, your journey to this coastal paradise begins with a smooth arrival.

Transportation within Clearwater

Exploring Clearwater's beaches, attractions, and vibrant neighborhoods is a breeze with a variety of transportation options at your disposal. Here's an extensive guide to help you navigate within Clearwater:

1. Car Rentals

Rental Agencies: Major car rental agencies operate in Clearwater, offering a convenient way to explore the city and its surroundings at your own pace.

Flexibility: Having a rental car provides flexibility for day trips, exploring nearby attractions, and reaching destinations not easily accessible by public transport.

2. Public Transportation

Pinellas Suncoast Transit Authority (PSTA):

- PSTA operates bus services covering Clearwater and the wider region.

- Bus routes connect key areas, attractions, and neighboring cities.

Fares and Passes: Purchase individual tickets or explore the cost-effective option of day passes for unlimited travel within a specified period.

3. Clearwater Ferry

Water Transportation: The Clearwater Ferry offers a scenic and efficient mode of transport between Clearwater Beach and downtown Clearwater.

Routes: Multiple routes connect popular spots, providing a unique perspective of the area from the water.

4. Rideshare Services

Uber and Lyft: Both Uber and Lyft operate in Clearwater, providing convenient rides within the city and surrounding areas.

Availability: Easily accessible via mobile apps, rideshare services are often readily available.

5. Biking and Walking

Bike Rentals: Explore Clearwater's scenic spots on two wheels by renting a bike from local shops.

Pedestrian-Friendly Areas: Downtown Clearwater and Clearwater Beach are pedestrian-friendly, making walking an enjoyable way to discover local attractions.

6. Taxis

Taxi Services: Taxis are available for on-demand transportation, especially in busy areas and at transportation hubs.

Taxi Stands: Find taxis at designated stands or request one via phone or mobile apps.

7. Airport Transportation

Shuttles and Transfers: Arrange airport transfers or shuttle services in advance for a seamless journey to and from Tampa International Airport or St. Pete-Clearwater International Airport.

Rental Cars: Rental car facilities are available at both airports for added convenience.

8. Scooter Rentals

Electric Scooters: Some areas may have electric scooter rental services, providing a fun and efficient way to cover short distances.

Safety: Follow local regulations and safety guidelines when using electric scooters.

9. Tips for Transportation

Traffic Considerations: Be mindful of traffic, especially during peak hours. Plan accordingly to avoid delays.

Parking: Check parking options and fees if you choose to rent a car. Some accommodations may provide parking facilities.

Schedule Awareness: Familiarize yourself with the schedules of buses, ferries, and other transportation services to optimize your time.

Local Guidance: Seek advice from locals or information centers for insights on the most efficient and enjoyable transportation options for your specific needs.

Clearwater's diverse transportation options cater to various preferences, making it easy to explore the city's gems. Whether you opt for the flexibility of a rental car, the scenic route on a ferry, or the convenience of rideshare services, each mode of transportation contributes to a memorable journey in this coastal paradise.

Detailed Accommodation Options in Clearwater

Clearwater welcomes visitors with a plethora of accommodation options ranging from luxurious beachfront resorts to cozy boutique hotels and budget-friendly motels. Here's an extensive guide to help you find the perfect place to stay during your Clearwater getaway:

1. Beachfront Resorts

Opulent Retreats: Clearwater Beach is adorned with upscale resorts offering stunning Gulf views, private beach access, and world-class amenities.

Notable Resorts: The Opal Sands Resort, Sandpearl Resort, and the Hyatt Regency Clearwater Beach Resort and Spa are among the luxurious options.

Amenities: Expect spas, fine dining, pools with cabanas, and direct access to the sugary sands.

- **Opal Sands Resort**

Address: 430 S Gulfview Blvd, Clearwater, FL 33767, United States
Phone Number: +1 727-450-0380
Price per Night: $394

- **Sandpearl Resort**

Address: 500 Mandalay Ave, Clearwater Beach, FL 33767, United States
Phone Number: +1 727-441-2425
Price per Night: **$252**

- **Hyatt Regency Clearwater Beach Resort**

Address: 301 S Gulfview Blvd, Clearwater Beach, FL 33767, United States
Phone Number: +1 727-373-1234
Price per Night: $217

2. Boutique Hotels

Unique Charm: Boutique hotels in Clearwater provide intimate and stylish accommodations, often with personalized service.

Options: The Winter the Dolphin's Beach Club, Edge Hotel Clearwater Beach, and the Barefoot Bay Resort and Marina offer distinct experiences.

Local Flavor: Enjoy local art, unique room designs, and personalized touches that reflect the character of Clearwater.

- ## Winter the Dolphin's Beach Club
  Address: 655 S Gulfview Blvd, Clearwater Beach, FL 33767, United States
  Phone Number: +1 727-228-8575
  Price per Night: $213

- ## Edge Hotel Clearwater Beach
  Address: 505 S Gulfview Blvd Ground Floor, Clearwater, FL 33767, United States

Phone Number: +1 727-281-3100
Price per Night: $218

- ## Barefoot Bay Resort and Marina
Address: 401 E Shore Dr, Clearwater, FL 33767, United States
Phone Number: +1 727-998-3611
Price per Night: $225

3. Chain Hotels

Reliable Comfort: Well-known chain hotels such as Marriott, Hilton, and Holiday Inn are present in Clearwater, offering consistency in service and amenities.

Options: Courtyard by Marriott, Hilton Clearwater Beach Resort & Spa, and Holiday Inn Hotel & Suites Clearwater Beach are popular choices.

Familiarity: Travelers often opt for chain hotels for their familiarity and loyalty programs.

- **Courtyard by Marriott**
Address: 455 East Shore Drive, Clearwater Beach, FL, 33767, US
Phone Number: +1 877-972-8116
Price per Night: $179

- **Hilton Clearwater Beach Resort & Spa**
Address: 400 Mandalay Ave, Clearwater, FL 33767, United States
Phone Number: +1 727-461-3222
Price per Night: $207

- **Holiday Inn Hotel & Suites Clearwater Beach**
Address: 521 S Gulfview Blvd, Clearwater Beach, FL 33767, United States
Phone Number: +1 727-447-6461
Price per Night: $401

4. Vacation Rentals

Home Away from Home: Vacation rentals, including condos and beachfront houses, provide a home-like atmosphere.

Platforms: Explore options on platforms like Airbnb and Vrbo for a variety of rentals catering to different group sizes and preferences.

Flexibility: Ideal for families or groups seeking more space and the ability to cook their own meals.

- **Airbnb**
Address: 400 Mandalay Ave, Clearwater, FL 33767
Phone Number: 17579977161
Price per Night: $20

5. Budget-Friendly Motels

Affordable Stays: Clearwater offers budget-friendly motels for travelers seeking economical accommodation.

Options: Pelican Pointe Hotel and Clearwater Beach Hotel are examples of motels that balance affordability with convenience.

Basic Amenities: Expect clean rooms, essential amenities, and proximity to attractions without breaking the bank.

- **Pelican Pointe Hotel**

Address: 445 S Gulfview Blvd, Clearwater Beach, FL 33767, United States
Phone Number: +1 727-441-4902
Price per Night: $162

6. Extended Stay Accommodations

Long-Term Convenience: Extended stay hotels cater to those planning an extended visit, offering kitchen facilities and additional living space.

Options: Residence Inn by Marriott and Candlewood Suites Clearwater provide comfort for longer stays.

Cost-Efficiency: Ideal for business travelers or those wanting a home-like environment during an extended vacation.

- **Residence Inn by Marriott**

Address: 940 COURT STREET, CLEARWATER, FLORIDA, USA, 33756
Phone Number: +1 877-562-5422
Price per Night: $161

7. Luxury Condos:

Residential Luxury: Some resorts and private entities offer luxury condos with full kitchens, multiple bedrooms, and expansive living areas.

Exclusivity: Enjoy the perks of resort-style living combined with the privacy of a residential setting.

Ideal for Groups: Perfect for families, larger groups, or those desiring a more exclusive experience.

8. Accessible Accommodations

Inclusive Options: Clearwater strives to provide accessible accommodations for travelers with mobility challenges.

Features: Look for hotels and resorts equipped with ramps, elevators, and accessible rooms.

Communication: Contact accommodations in advance to ensure specific accessibility needs are met.

9. Pet-Friendly Stays:

Furry Friends Welcome: For those traveling with pets, Clearwater offers pet-friendly accommodations.

Policies: Check each hotel's pet policy, and consider options like Kimpton Hotel Zamora, which is known for its pet-friendly approach.

Dog-Friendly Beaches: Explore Clearwater's dog-friendly beaches for a well-rounded experience.

10. Tips for Booking Accommodations

Book in Advance: Secure your preferred accommodation by booking well in advance, especially during peak seasons.

Read Reviews: Explore guest reviews on various platforms for insights into the experiences of previous visitors.

Consider Location: Choose accommodations based on your preferences, whether it's beachfront access, proximity to attractions, or a quieter residential area.

Check Amenities: Review the amenities offered by each accommodation to ensure they align with your expectations.

Clearwater's diverse accommodation options cater to every traveler's needs, ensuring a comfortable and memorable stay in this coastal paradise. Whether you're seeking a lavish resort experience, a charming boutique stay, or budget-friendly comfort, Clearwater has the perfect lodging option for your getaway.

CHAPTER FOUR

Banks, Currency and Payment Methods

A Comprehensive Guide to Banks, Currency, and Payment Methods.

As you embark on your Clearwater adventure, understanding the financial landscape is crucial. Here's an extensive guide to banks, currency, and payment methods to ensure smooth transactions during your stay:

1. Currency

U.S. Dollar (USD): The official currency in Clearwater is the United States Dollar. Cash is widely accepted, and credit/debit cards are commonly used for transactions.

2. Banks and ATMs

Major Banks: Clearwater is home to various major banks, including Wells Fargo, Bank of America, Chase, and local banks such as Achieva Credit Union.

ATM Accessibility: ATMs are plentiful and can be found at banks, shopping centers, and tourist areas. Ensure your card is compatible with international withdrawals.

Banking Hours: Typical banking hours are Monday to Friday, 9:00 AM to 5:00 PM. On Saturdays, some branches may offer limited services.

3. Credit and Debit Cards

Wide Acceptance: Credit and debit cards are widely accepted at most establishments, including hotels, restaurants, shops, and attractions.

International Fees: Check with your bank regarding international transaction fees and inform them of your travel dates to avoid any card-related issues.

Chip-and-PIN: While chip-and-PIN cards are becoming more common, many places still accept traditional magnetic stripe cards.

4. Traveler's Checks

Declining Usage: Traveler's checks are becoming less common, and many businesses may not accept them. It's advisable to rely on cards and cash.

Exchange Services: If you plan to use traveler's checks, check with local banks for exchange services.

5. Mobile Payments

Contactless Payments: Mobile payment methods like Apple Pay, Google Pay, and Samsung Pay are increasingly accepted at various establishments.

NFC Technology: Ensure your smartphone has NFC technology, and check for the acceptance of mobile payments at the places you visit.

6. Currency Exchange

Limited Need: As the U.S. Dollar is the local currency, there is limited need for currency exchange services.

Airports and Banks: If required, currency exchange services can be found at airports and major banks.

7. Tips for Financial Transactions

Inform Your Bank: Notify your bank about your travel dates and destination to prevent any potential issues with your cards.

Carry Some Cash: While cards are widely accepted, having some cash on hand for small purchases and places that may not accept cards is advisable.

Check for Fees: Be aware of potential fees associated with currency conversion, ATM withdrawals, and international transactions.

Emergency Contact Numbers: Keep a record of your bank's emergency contact numbers in case you encounter any issues with your cards.

8. Financial Safety

Secure Transactions: Use reputable ATMs and be cautious when entering PINs. Shield your PIN from onlookers.

Fraud Alerts: Keep an eye on your bank statements for any unauthorized transactions, and report any issues promptly.

Secure Your Belongings: Ensure the safety of your cards and cash by using secure wallets or money belts.

Clearwater's financial infrastructure ensures a seamless experience for travelers, with various options for managing transactions. Whether you prefer the convenience of cards, the security of traveler's checks, or the simplicity of cash, you'll find suitable solutions to meet your financial needs in this coastal paradise.

CHAPTER FIVE

Things to See, Do and Avoid

Top Tourist Attractions in Clearwater

Clearwater boasts a captivating blend of pristine beaches, vibrant cultural spots, and outdoor adventures. Here's an extensive guide to the top tourist attractions in Clearwater, ensuring you experience the best this coastal paradise has to offer:

1. Clearwater Beach

Address: 455 East Shore Drive, Clearwater Beach, Florida, USA, 33767
Phone Number: +1 727-442-4770

Sugary Sands: Renowned for its powdery white sands and clear turquoise waters, Clearwater Beach consistently ranks among the best beaches globally.

Pier 60: A hub of activity, Pier 60 offers daily sunset celebrations, a fishing pier, street performers, and a lively atmosphere.

Water Activities: Enjoy water sports like jet-skiing, parasailing, and paddleboarding, or simply relax under the Florida sun.

2. Clearwater Marine Aquarium

Address: 249 Windward Passage, Clearwater, FL 33767, USA
Phone Number: +1 727-491-7318

Home of Winter: Known worldwide as the home of Winter the Dolphin, the Clearwater Marine Aquarium focuses on marine life rescue, rehabilitation, and education.

Interactive Exhibits: Explore interactive exhibits, watch marine animal presentations, and learn about the center's conservation efforts.

3. Sand Key Park

Address: 1060 Gulf Blvd, Clearwater, FL 33767, United States
Phone Number: +1 727-588-4852

Natural Retreat: Sand Key Park offers a quieter beach experience with nature trails, picnic areas, and stunning views of the Gulf of Mexico.

Wildlife Spotting: Birdwatching is popular here, and you might encounter sea turtles and dolphins along the shoreline.

4. Caladesi Island State Park

Address: 1 Causeway Blvd, Dunedin, FL 34698, United States
Phone Number: +1 727-469-5918

Natural Beauty: Accessible by ferry or private boat, Caladesi Island State Park features untouched beaches, nature trails, and opportunities for shelling.

Secluded Paradise: Enjoy the serenity of this barrier island, known for its pristine landscapes and abundant wildlife.

5. Honeymoon Island State Park

Address: 1 Causeway Blvd. Dunedin, Florida 34698
Phone Number: +1 727-241-6106

Nature Escapes: Honeymoon Island State Park offers nature trails, birdwatching, and a pet-friendly beach, providing a tranquil escape.

Shelling Paradise: Collect seashells along the shoreline or explore the Rotary Centennial Nature Center for more insights into the area's ecology.

6. Moccasin Lake Nature Park

Address: 2750 Park Trail Ln, Clearwater, FL 33759, United States
Phone Numbe: +1 727-562-4315

Educational Nature Park: Moccasin Lake Nature Park provides a peaceful setting with walking trails, a butterfly garden, and educational programs about local wildlife.

Boardwalk Exploration: Wander along the boardwalks that meander through the park, offering glimpses of native flora and fauna.

7. Coachman Park

Address: Drew St, Clearwater, FL 33755, United States
Phone Number: +1 727-562-4800

Events and Festivals: Coachman Park is a central venue for events and festivals, hosting concerts, cultural celebrations, and the annual Clearwater Jazz Holiday.

Waterfront Setting: Situated along the waterfront, it provides a scenic backdrop for various activities.

8. Ruth Eckerd Hall

Address: 1111 McMullen Booth Rd, Clearwater, FL 33759, United States
Phone Number: +1 727-791-7400

Cultural Hub: Ruth Eckerd Hall is a premier performing arts venue, hosting concerts, Broadway shows, and cultural performances.

Artistic Excellence: Check the schedule for world-class performances spanning various genres.

9. Sunsets at Pier 60 Festival

Address: 1 Causeway Blvd, Clearwater, FL 33767, United States
Phone Number: +1 727-871-8060

Daily Celebration: The Sunsets at Pier 60 Festival is a daily celebration featuring artisans, street performers, and live music against the backdrop of the setting sun.

Local Artisans: Browse through local art vendors and enjoy the lively atmosphere as the day comes to a close.

10. Downtown Clearwater

Address: 600 Cleveland St., Suite 600
Clearwater, FL 33755
Phone Number: +1 727-222-3258

Historic Charm: Explore the historic downtown area with its charming streets, local shops, and a variety of dining options.

Cleveland Street District: The Cleveland Street District is a hub for entertainment, dining, and cultural experiences.

11. Ybor City

Address: 25 Causeway Boulevard slip 8, Clearwater Beach, FL 33767, United States
Phone Number: +1 727-442-7600

Historical District: While not in Clearwater, Ybor City in nearby Tampa is worth a visit. Known for its historic architecture, Ybor City offers a lively atmosphere with shops, restaurants, and nightlife.

Cigar Heritage: Learn about Tampa's cigar industry heritage and stroll along Seventh Avenue's vibrant streets.

12. Tarpon Springs Sponge Docks

Address: 735 Dodecanese Blvd, Tarpon Springs, FL 34689, United States
Phone Number: +1 760-276-3899

Greek Influence: Explore the Greek-influenced community of Tarpon Springs, known for its sponge docks, Greek cuisine, and waterfront charm.

Sponge Diving History: Learn about the history of sponge diving and shop for natural sponges and unique gifts.

13. Safety Harbor Spa and Philippe Park

Address: 105 N Bayshore Dr, Safety Harbor, FL 34695, United States
Phone Number: +1 727-726-1161

Relaxation and History: Safety Harbor Spa offers a rejuvenating experience, while Philippe Park provides a historic setting with Indian mounds and scenic views.

Outdoor Exploration: Walk or bike through Philippe Park's trails, discovering the area's Native American history.

14. Dunedin Historical Society and Museum

Address: 349 Main St, Dunedin, FL 34698-5700
Phone Number: +1 727-736-1176

Preserving History: Explore Dunedin's history at the Dunedin Historical Society and Museum, housed in a former railroad station.

Local Artifacts: View exhibits showcasing local artifacts, photographs, and the development of the area.

Clearwater's diverse attractions cater to a range of interests, from sun-soaked beaches and marine life encounters to cultural performances and historical explorations. Whether you seek relaxation, adventure, or a bit of both, Clearwater invites you to discover its treasures along Florida's Gulf Coast.

Off the Beaten Path Experiences in Clearwater

For those seeking to venture beyond the well-trodden paths and discover the hidden gems of Clearwater, here's a guide to off-the-beaten-path experiences that promise a unique and authentic exploration of this coastal haven:

1. Dunedin Hammock Park

Address: 1900 San Mateo Dr, Dunedin, FL 34698, United States
Phone Number: +1 727-812-4530

Nature Retreat: Escape to the tranquility of Dunedin Hammock Park, a lesser-known nature reserve offering hiking trails, birdwatching opportunities, and a serene ambiance.

Elevated Boardwalks: Wander through elevated boardwalks that wind through the park's diverse ecosystems, providing glimpses of Florida's native flora and fauna.

2. Philippe Park Indian Mound Trail

Address: 2525 Philippe Pkwy, Safety Harbor, FL 34695, United States

Phone Number: **(727) 582-2100**

Historical Hike: Explore the Indian Mound Trail within Philippe Park for a blend of history and nature. The trail winds through ancient Native American burial mounds and offers picturesque views of Old Tampa Bay.

Oak Trees and Wildlife: Admire the majestic live oak trees, and keep an eye out for wildlife, including birds and possibly even dolphins in the bay.

3. Dolphin Trail Kayak Adventure

Address: 2824 47th St S, Gulfport, FL 33711, United States
Phone Number: **+1 727-224-0164**

Hidden Waterways: Embark on a kayak adventure along the less-explored waterways around Clearwater. Several local companies offer guided tours, providing a chance to paddle through mangroves and spot dolphins in their natural habitat.

Educational Experience: Some tours include educational insights into marine life and ecosystems, offering a unique perspective on Clearwater's coastal environment.

4. Murals of Dunedin

Phone Number: +1 727-462-2840

Artistic Exploration: Stroll through the streets of Dunedin to discover an array of vibrant murals adorning the town's buildings. These murals, often tucked away in unexpected corners, showcase local artistry and the community's creative spirit.

Self-Guided Tour: Create your own self-guided mural tour, capturing the essence of Dunedin's artistic expression.

5. Lake Tarpon

Address: 37061 US Hwy 19 N, Palm Harbor, FL 34684, United States
Phone Number: +1 727-937-8412

Hidden Gem for Fishing: Lake Tarpon, nestled away from the bustling tourist areas, is a haven for fishing enthusiasts. Rent a boat or join a local guide for a peaceful day of freshwater fishing.

Scenic Beauty: Surrounded by cypress trees and lush greenery, Lake Tarpon provides a serene escape with opportunities to spot various bird species.

6. Florida Botanical Gardens

Address: 12520 Ulmerton Rd, Largo, FL 33774, United States
Phone Number: +1 727-753-7837

Botanical Oasis: While not entirely off the beaten path, the Florida Botanical Gardens offer a quieter escape compared to the beaches. Wander through themed gardens, including tropical, butterfly, and native plant displays.

Photography Haven: Capture the beauty of blooming flowers, butterflies, and scenic landscapes in this hidden oasis.

7. Honeymoon Island Nature Trails

Address: 423 Lafayette Blvd, Oldsmar, FL 34677, USA
Phone Number: +1 813-448-5635

Secluded Exploration: Beyond the main beach area of Honeymoon Island, discover the lesser-known nature trails. These trails meander through coastal habitats, providing a peaceful escape.

Birding Opportunities: Birdwatchers will appreciate the diverse avian species that inhabit the island, from ospreys to shorebirds.

8. Keystone Road Scenic Drive

Address: 25 Causeway Blvd, Clearwater Beach, FL 33767, USA
Phone Number: +1 727-724-4299

Rural Serenity: Take a scenic drive along Keystone Road, offering a glimpse into the rural side of Clearwater. This less-traveled route takes you through picturesque landscapes, including farms and open fields.

Picnic Spots: Pack a picnic and stop at one of the quiet spots along the way for a relaxing break surrounded by nature.

9. Safety Harbor Art and Music Center

Address: 706 2nd St N, Safety Harbor, FL 34695, USA
Phone Number: +1 727-725-4018

Hidden Cultural Gem: Visit the Safety Harbor Art and Music Center for a dose of local arts and culture. This intimate venue hosts live performances, art exhibits, and workshops.

Community Engagement: Immerse yourself in the local creative scene and perhaps catch an up-and-coming artist's showcase.

10. Moccasin Lake Nature Park Boardwalk

Address: 2750 Park Trail Ln, Clearwater, FL 33759, USA
Phone Number: +1 727-562-4315

Boardwalk Immersion: While Moccasin Lake Nature Park is known, its extensive boardwalk system provides an immersive journey through wetlands and natural habitats.

Birdwatching Haven: Birdwatchers will be delighted by the variety of bird species that call this park home.

11. Congo River Golf

Address: 20060 US Hwy 19 N, Clearwater, FL 33764, USA
Phone Number: +1 727-797-4222

Adventure Golf: For a quirky and entertaining experience, try your hand at adventure golf at Congo River Golf. Navigate mini-golf courses surrounded by lush landscaping, waterfalls, and even encounter live alligators.

Family-Friendly Fun: Ideal for families or those looking for a lighthearted and unique outdoor activity.

12. Downtown Palm Harbor Historic District

Address: 1190 Georgia Ave, Palm Harbor, FL 34683, USA
Phone Number: +1 727-787-4700

Historical Charm: Explore the historic district of Downtown Palm Harbor, featuring charming architecture, local shops, and a laid-back atmosphere.

Local Eateries: Enjoy a meal at one of the local eateries for an authentic taste of the community.

Clearwater's off-the-beaten-path experiences promise a deeper connection with the area's nature, culture, and hidden treasures. Whether you choose to paddle through secluded waterways, explore historic trails, or discover artistic expressions in unexpected corners, these experiences offer a richer understanding of Clearwater's diverse offerings beyond its famous beaches.

Outdoor Activities in Clearwater

Clearwater's sun-drenched landscapes and coastal charm provide the perfect backdrop for a myriad of outdoor adventures. Whether you're a beach enthusiast, nature lover, or thrill-seeker, this guide explores the diverse outdoor activities awaiting you in this coastal paradise:

1. Clearwater Beach

Sun-soaked Relaxation:Clearwater Beach is a haven for sun worshippers. Sink your toes into the powdery white sand, bask in the Florida sun, and take in the breathtaking views of the Gulf of Mexico.

Waterfront Dining: Explore beachside cafes and restaurants offering fresh seafood and panoramic views of the turquoise waters.

Sunset Celebrations: Join the daily Sunset at Pier 60 Festival for a vibrant atmosphere with street performers, artisans, and live music as the sun dips below the horizon.

2. Water Sports Extravaganza

Jet Skiing: Feel the thrill of skimming across the waves on a jet ski, available for rental at various locations.

Parasailing: Soar high above the Gulf waters for a unique perspective of Clearwater Beach. Parasailing operators offer a bird's-eye view of the coastline.

Paddleboarding and Kayaking: Explore the calm waters near the shore by paddle boarding or kayaking. For both beginners and experienced paddlers, rentals and guided tours are available.

3. Fishing Adventures

Deep-Sea Fishing: Charter a boat for a deep-sea fishing excursion. Clearwater is known for its abundant marine life, offering opportunities to catch grouper, snapper, and even shark.

Pier Fishing: Enjoy a more laid-back fishing experience at one of the area's fishing piers, such as Pier 60 or the Clearwater Beach Fishing Pier.

4. Dolphin Watching Tours

Marine Encounters: Set sail on a dolphin-watching tour to witness these playful creatures in their natural habitat. Many tours also provide insights into the local marine ecosystem.

Sailing Cruises: Explore the Gulf waters on a sailing cruise, offering a serene and environmentally friendly way to enjoy the coastal scenery.

5. Nature Trails and Parks

Moccasin Lake Nature Park: Wander through Moccasin Lake Nature Park's boardwalks and trails, immersing yourself in the natural beauty of wetlands and wooded areas.

Philippe Park Indian Mound Trail: Explore the historical Indian Mound Trail in Philippe Park, blending history with nature as you stroll along the bay.

6. Biking Adventures

Pinellas Trail: Embark on a biking adventure along the Pinellas Trail, a 38-mile-long trail passing through Clearwater. Rent bikes locally for a leisurely ride through scenic landscapes.

Bike Rentals: Various bike rental shops offer a range of options, from cruiser bikes for a relaxed beachside ride to mountain bikes for off-road exploration.

7. Golfing in the Sun

Countryside Country Club: Tee off at the Countryside Country Club, featuring an 18-hole golf course surrounded by lush landscapes.

Innisbrook Golf Resort: For a premier golf experience, visit the Innisbrook Golf Resort, home to the PGA Tour's Valspar Championship.

8. Stand-Up Paddleboarding (SUP) Yoga

Mindful Waters: Combine the serenity of yoga with the balancing act of stand-up paddleboarding. SUP yoga classes are offered in calm waterways for a unique outdoor wellness experience.

Guided Sessions: Join guided sessions suitable for all levels, including beginners.

9. Tandem Skydiving

Adrenaline Rush: Experience the ultimate thrill with tandem skydiving. Clearwater offers breathtaking aerial views as you freefall from thousands of feet above.

Certified Operators: Choose from certified skydiving operators who prioritize safety and provide an unforgettable adventure.

10. Camping at Fort De Soto Park

Seaside Camping: Fort De Soto Park offers seaside camping opportunities, allowing you to wake up to the sound of waves and enjoy the pristine surroundings.

Nature Trails: Explore nature trails, kayak through mangrove tunnels, and savor the beauty of this coastal park.

11. Sunset Sails and Dinner Cruises

Romantic Evenings: Embark on a romantic sunset sail or dinner cruise, enjoying the changing colors of the sky over the Gulf. Many operators offer onboard dining experiences.

Live Entertainment: Some cruises feature live entertainment, creating a memorable evening under the stars.

12. Kayaking through Mangrove Tunnels

Eco-Adventure: Delve into the unique ecosystems of mangrove tunnels on a guided kayak tour. Paddle through winding waterways and witness the diverse marine life that calls these areas home.

Educational Excursion: Knowledgeable guides often share insights into the importance of mangrove habitats and conservation efforts.

13. Caldwell Nature Preserve

Hidden Gem: Explore the Caldwell Nature Preserve, a hidden gem offering walking trails, butterfly gardens, and a chance to observe local wildlife.

Educational Programs: Check for any scheduled educational programs or events hosted by the preserve.

14. Palm Pavilion Beachside Grill & Bar

Beachside Dining: Indulge in a unique dining experience at Palm Pavilion, located directly on Clearwater Beach. Enjoy fresh seafood and tropical drinks while soaking in the ocean views.

Live Music: Some evenings feature live music, adding to the laid-back atmosphere.

15. Beach Volleyball

Sand Sports: Join a beach volleyball game at Clearwater Beach. Several areas provide nets for casual play, and some beachfront establishments host organized tournaments.

Social Sports: Engage in the lively social scene of beach sports, meeting fellow enthusiasts and enjoying the coastal setting.

Clearwater's outdoor activities offer something for everyone, from adrenaline-pumping adventures to serene nature escapes. Whether you prefer the thrill of water sports, the tranquility of nature trails, or the laid-back atmosphere of beachside activities, Clearwater invites you to embrace the sunshine and create unforgettable outdoor memories along Florida's Gulf Coast.

Cultural Experience in Clearwater

Clearwater, beyond its stunning beaches, embraces a rich cultural tapestry waiting to be explored:

Dunedin Historical Society and Museum: Immerse yourself in the history of the region at the Dunedin Historical Society and Museum, housed in a former railroad station. Discover artifacts, photographs, and exhibits showcasing the development of the area.

Ruth Eckerd Hall: Delve into the cultural scene at Ruth Eckerd Hall, a premier performing arts venue hosting concerts, Broadway shows, and cultural performances. Check the schedule for a diverse range of artistic expressions.

Ybor City in Tampa: While not within Clearwater, a visit to Ybor City in Tampa offers a unique cultural experience. Known for its historical architecture, this district boasts a vibrant atmosphere with shops, restaurants, and a nod to Tampa's cigar industry heritage.

Tarpon Springs Sponge Docks: Explore the Greek-influenced community of Tarpon Springs, famous for its sponge docks. Immerse yourself in Greek culture, savor authentic cuisine, and learn about the history of sponge diving.

Events and Festivals in Clearwater

Clearwater comes alive with a variety of events and festivals throughout the year:

Clearwater Jazz Holiday: Join the annual Clearwater Jazz Holiday, a renowned event featuring world-class musicians and a vibrant atmosphere. The festival takes place at Coachman Park, providing a perfect setting for music enthusiasts.

Sunsets at Pier 60 Festival: Experience the daily Sunsets at Pier 60 Festival. This free event celebrates the setting sun with street performers, artisans, and live music, creating a lively atmosphere along Clearwater Beach.

Clearwater Sea-Blues Festival: If you're a fan of blues music, don't miss the Clearwater Sea-Blues Festival. This event showcases talented blues artists against the backdrop of Clearwater's coastal charm.

Palm Pavilion Beachside Grill & Bar Events: Check out events at Palm Pavilion, a beachside establishment offering live music and a relaxed atmosphere. Enjoy the sounds of local musicians while savoring coastal cuisine.

Family-Friendly Activities in Clearwater

Clearwater is a haven for family-friendly adventures and attractions:

Marine Aquarium Clearwater: Marine Aquarium Clearwater is the home to Winter the Dolphin. This family-friendly attraction focuses on marine life rescue and rehabilitation, offering educational programs and interactive exhibits.

Pier 60 Playground: Enjoy family time at the Pier 60 Playground, located on Clearwater Beach. Let the kids play in the sand, and take advantage of the nearby amenities and picnic areas.

Congo River Golf: Embark on a family-friendly adventure at Congo River Golf. Putt through mini-golf courses surrounded by waterfalls, lush landscaping, and encounter live alligators along the way.

Safety Harbor Art and Music Center: Engage in artistic experiences at the Safety Harbor Art and Music Center. This venue hosts family-friendly events, workshops, and performances, creating a cultural haven for all ages.

Itinerary Plan in Clearwater

Crafting a well-rounded itinerary ensures you make the most of your Clearwater experience:

Day 1 - Beach Bliss

Morning: Start with a relaxing morning at Clearwater Beach. Enjoy the soft sands and take a stroll along the iconic Pier 60.

Afternoon: Savor seafood at a beachfront restaurant.

Evening: Join the Sunset at Pier 60 Festival for live music and street performances.

Day 2 - Cultural Exploration

Morning: Visit the Dunedin Historical Society and Museum for a dose of local history.

Afternoon: Head to Ruth Eckerd Hall for a matinee performance or explore the vibrant Dunedin murals.

Evening: Choose a local eatery in downtown Dunedin for dinner.

Day 3 - Nature and Adventure

Morning: Explore Moccasin Lake Nature Park's trails and boardwalks.

Afternoon: Enjoy water sports at Clearwater Beach or take a dolphin-watching tour.

Evening: Dine at a beachside restaurant for a taste of coastal cuisine.

Things to Avoid in Clearwater

While Clearwater is a fantastic destination, being aware of potential pitfalls can enhance your experience:

Avoid Peak Crowds: If possible, plan your visit during off-peak seasons to avoid crowded beaches and attractions.

Be Mindful of Wildlife: While marine life is a highlight, avoid approaching or feeding wild animals. Respect their natural habitats.

Watch for Traffic: Clearwater can experience heavy traffic, especially during peak times. Plan your transportation and explore local transportation options to avoid delays.

Be Cautious with Water Activities: Follow safety guidelines when engaging in water activities. Pay attention to local advisories and weather conditions for a safe experience.

Watch for Stingrays: Stingrays may be present in shallow waters. Shuffle your feet when walking in the ocean to avoid stepping on them.

Beware of Sunburn: Florida sun can be intense. Apply sunscreen, stay hydrated, and seek shade during the hottest part of the day to avoid sunburn.

Being mindful of these considerations ensures a smoother and more enjoyable experience in Clearwater, allowing you to make the most of this coastal paradise while avoiding potential pitfalls.

CHAPTER SIX

Eating and Drinking in Clearwater

Restaurants in Clearwater

Clearwater's dining scene is a delectable fusion of fresh seafood, international flavors, and vibrant atmospheres. Embark on a culinary journey as we explore the diverse range of restaurants that define the gastronomic landscape of this coastal paradise:

1. Columbia Restaurant
Address: 1241 Gulf Blvd, Clearwater, FL 33767, United States
Phone Number: +1 727-596-8400

Spanish Flair: Step into the historic charm of the Columbia Restaurant, known for its

Spanish-inspired cuisine. Enjoy paella, tapas, and sangria in a setting that reflects the rich heritage of Ybor City.

Charming Ambiance: The restaurant's ambiance, with its flamenco dancers and intricate tilework, transports diners to the heart of Spain.

2. Frenchy's Clearwater Beach Restaurants

Address: 7 Rockaway St, Clearwater, FL 33767, United States
Phone Number: +1 727-446-4844

Seafood Paradise: Frenchy's has become synonymous with Clearwater's seafood scene. Indulge in fresh catches of the day, including their famous grouper sandwiches, at one of the various Frenchy's establishments along Clearwater Beach.

Beachfront Vibes: With beachfront locations, you can dine with your toes in the sand and savor the Gulf breeze.

3. Palm Pavilion Beachside Grill & Bar

Address: 10 Bay Esplanade, Clearwater, FL 33767, United States
Phone Number: +1 727-446-2642

Oceanfront Dining: Located directly on Clearwater Beach, Palm Pavilion offers a casual yet refined dining experience with oceanfront views.

Live Music: Enjoy live music during select evenings, enhancing the laid-back atmosphere.

4. Bob Heilman's Beachcomber

Address: 447 Mandalay Ave, Clearwater Beach, FL 33767, United States
Phone Number: +1 727-442-4144

Classic Elegance: Bob Heilman's Beachcomber is a classic choice for those seeking an elegant dining experience. Known for its prime steaks and seafood, this restaurant exudes timeless charm.

Upscale Dining: The intimate setting makes it an ideal choice for a special evening out.

5. Sea-Guini at Opal Sands Resort

Address: 430 S Gulfview Blvd, Clearwater, FL 33767, United States
Phone Number: +1 727-450-6236

Gulf-to-Table Concept: Sea-Guini offers a Gulf-to-table dining experience within the Opal Sands Resort. Indulge in a menu featuring locally sourced seafood and Italian-inspired dishes.

Panoramic Views: Enjoy panoramic views of the Gulf of Mexico from the modern and stylish setting.

6. Clear Sky Cafe

Address: 490 Mandalay Ave Ste 1, Clearwater, FL 33767, United States
Phone Number: +1 727-442-3684

Eclectic Menu: Clear Sky Cafe boasts an eclectic menu, offering everything from sushi and seafood to comfort food classics.

Vibrant Atmosphere: The vibrant and artsy ambiance adds to the appeal of this downtown Clearwater gem.

7. Caretta on the Gulf

Address: 500 Mandalay Ave, Clearwater Beach, FL 33767, United States
Phone Number: +1 727-674-4171

Fine Dining by the Water: Located in the Sandpearl Resort, Caretta on the Gulf offers fine dining with a focus on fresh, locally sourced ingredients.

Oceanfront Terrace: Dine on the oceanfront terrace for an elegant experience with breathtaking sunset views.

8. Cork & Brew Bistro

Address: 482 Poinsettia Ave, Clearwater Beach, FL 33767, United States
Phone Number: +1 727-474-0578

Craft Beer Pairings: Cork & Brew Bistro is a haven for beer enthusiasts, offering a diverse selection of craft beers paired with a menu featuring globally inspired dishes.

Casual and Relaxed: The casual setting makes it a great spot for a laid-back meal with friends.

9. Bait House Tackle and Tavern
Address: 45 Causeway Blvd, Clearwater, FL 33767, United States
Phone Number: +1 727-446-8134

Quintessential Waterfront Spot: Nestled on the Clearwater Marina, Bait House Tackle and Tavern provides a quintessential waterfront dining experience.

Seafood Specialties: Sample their seafood specialties and enjoy the lively marina atmosphere.

10. Forlini's Ristorante and Bar
Address: 435 Mandalay Ave, Clearwater Beach, FL 33767, United States
Phone Number: +1 727-441-1111

Authentic Italian Flavors: Forlini's brings authentic Italian flavors to Clearwater. From pasta dishes to hearty mains, indulge in the robust tastes of Italy.

Cozy Setting: The cozy and welcoming ambiance adds to the overall dining experience.

11. Marina Cantina

Address: 25 Causeway Blvd, Clearwater, FL 33767, United States
Phone Number: +1 727-443-1750

Mexican-Inspired Delights: Marina Cantina offers a Mexican-inspired menu with a Gulf Coast twist. From tacos to ceviche, enjoy a fusion of flavors in a lively setting.

Waterfront Patio: Take advantage of the waterfront patio for a scenic meal.

12. Clearwater Wine Bar & Bistro

Address: 482 Poinsettia Ave, Clearwater Beach, FL 33767, United States
Phone Number: +1 727-446-8805

Wine Enthusiast Haven: If you appreciate wine, the Clearwater Wine Bar & Bistro is a must-visit. Pair your favorite wine with delectable dishes in a cozy, intimate setting.

Wine Selection: Explore their extensive wine selection, with knowledgeable staff to guide you through the options.

13. Rusty's Bistro at Sheraton Sand Key Resort

Address: 1160 Gulf Blvd, Clearwater Beach, FL 33767, United States
Phone Number: +1 727-595-1611

Contemporary Dining: Rusty's Bistro offers contemporary dining within the Sheraton Sand Key Resort. Indulge in a menu featuring fresh, local ingredients with a focus on sustainability.

Lush Outdoor Patio: Dine on the lush outdoor patio for a delightful al fresco experience.

14. Bascom's Chop House

Address: 3665 Ulmerton Rd, Clearwater, FL 33762, United States
Phone Number: +1 727-573-3363

Steakhouse Excellence: For those craving a classic steakhouse experience, Bascom's Chop House delivers with prime cuts and a sophisticated atmosphere.

Fine Dining Setting: The fine dining setting makes it an excellent choice for a special occasion.

15. Kiku Japanese Restaurant

Address: 483 Mandalay Ave #214, Clearwater, FL 33767, United States
Phone Number: +1 727-461-2633

Authentic Japanese Cuisine: Kiku Japanese Restaurant is a haven for sushi and Japanese cuisine enthusiasts. Delight in expertly crafted sushi rolls, sashimi, and traditional dishes.

Elegant Interior: The elegant interior adds to the overall dining experience.

Clearwater's restaurants cater to diverse tastes, ensuring a culinary adventure that mirrors the region's cultural richness and coastal allure. From seafood shacks with toes-in-the-sand vibes to upscale steakhouses with panoramic views, every dining experience in Clearwater is a celebration of the vibrant flavors that define Florida's Gulf Coast.

Street Food in Clearwater

Clearwater's streets come alive with an array of tempting street food options, offering a quick and flavorful way to savor local bites:

Pier 60 Sunset Festival: Explore the Pier 60 Sunset Festival, where local vendors offer street food delights during the nightly celebration. Indulge in everything from freshly popped kettle corn to coconut shrimp.

Food Trucks on Cleveland Street: Wander along Cleveland Street in downtown Clearwater, where you'll often find food trucks offering diverse street food options. From tacos to gourmet sandwiches, there's a culinary treat for every palate.

Beachfront Snack Shacks: Clearwater Beach boasts charming snack shacks right on the sand. Grab a quick bite like a beachside hot dog or a tropical fruit smoothie as you enjoy the sun and surf.

Downtown Clearwater Farmers Market: Visit the Downtown Clearwater Farmers Market for a taste of local street food. From empanadas to artisanal ice cream, the market offers a delightful mix of flavors.

Local Cuisine and Food Specialties in Clearwater

Clearwater's culinary scene is infused with flavors that capture the essence of the Gulf Coast. Dive into local cuisine and savor unique food specialties:

Grouper Sandwich: A quintessential Gulf Coast dish, the grouper sandwich is a local favorite. Head to seafood shacks like Frenchy's to enjoy this iconic sandwich, featuring fresh grouper fillets.

Stone Crab Claws: Indulge in the delicacy of stone crab claws, a seasonal treat available from October to May. These succulent claws are often served with tangy mustard sauce.

Florida Key Lime Pie: Satiate your sweet tooth with a slice of Florida Key Lime Pie. Creamy, tart, and refreshing, this dessert is a must-try, and many local establishments offer their own spin on this classic.

Conch Fritters: Venture beyond traditional seafood dishes and try conch fritters. These savory fritters feature chopped conch meat, herbs, and spices, offering a taste of the Caribbean.

Cuban Sandwich: Embrace the Cuban influence in Florida with a classic Cuban sandwich. Layers of ham, roast pork, Swiss cheese, pickles, mustard, and sometimes salami come together in a pressed delight.

Dietary Restrictions and Tips in Clearwater

Navigating dietary restrictions in Clearwater is manageable with a few helpful tips:

Seafood Sensations: Clearwater is renowned for its seafood, making it a haven for seafood lovers. However, if you have allergies or dietary restrictions, be sure to communicate your needs to restaurant staff.

Vegan and Vegetarian Options: Many restaurants offer vegan and vegetarian options, especially in downtown Clearwater and along Cleveland Street. Look for establishments that highlight plant-based choices on their menus.

Gluten-Free Friendly: Gluten-free dining is also accessible in Clearwater. Some restaurants provide gluten-free menus or are willing to accommodate gluten-free requests. Clear communication with waitstaff is key.

Farmers Markets and Local Produce: Explore farmers markets for fresh, local produce. This is an excellent option for those with dietary restrictions who prefer to prepare their own meals or snacks.

Check Menus in Advance: Prior to dining out, check restaurant menus online to get a sense of available options. Many establishments provide detailed menus on their websites, making it easier to plan according to dietary needs.

Popular Beverages and Nightlife in Clearwater

As the sun sets, Clearwater transforms into a vibrant nightlife destination with a diverse array of beverages and entertainment options:

Craft Beer Scene: Clearwater's craft beer scene is thriving. Explore local breweries and taprooms offering a variety of craft brews. Pair your beer with live music at some establishments for a complete experience.

Tropical Cocktails: Embrace the tropical vibes with refreshing cocktails. Many beachside bars and resorts specialize in crafting fruity concoctions that perfectly complement the coastal setting.

Rooftop Bars with Gulf Views: Enjoy panoramic views of the Gulf of Mexico from rooftop bars. These venues often feature a mix of handcrafted cocktails, live music, and a laid-back atmosphere.

Wine Bars: Wine enthusiasts can explore the city's wine bars, offering curated selections and often providing cozy environments for intimate conversations.

Beachfront Entertainment: Several beachfront establishments offer a dynamic nightlife scene. From dance floors to beach bonfires, you'll find a variety of entertainment options that extend into the late hours.

Live Music Venues: Clearwater is home to numerous live music venues, ranging from intimate bars to larger concert spaces. Check the local event calendar for performances by both local and touring artists.

Casual Beach Bars: Unwind at casual beach bars where you can sink your toes in the sand while enjoying a cold drink. These spots often host live music, creating a relaxed and enjoyable atmosphere.

Late-Night Eateries: For those seeking a post-midnight snack, explore late-night eateries that offer a variety of bites to satisfy your cravings.

Clearwater's nightlife caters to diverse tastes, whether you're looking for a laid-back beachfront experience, live music, or the excitement of a dance floor. From craft beers to tropical cocktails, the city's beverage scene complements the lively atmosphere, ensuring that your evenings in Clearwater are as memorable as the sun-soaked days.

CHAPTER SEVEN

Practical Information

Local Etiquette and Customs in Clearwater

Navigating local etiquette and customs enhances your experience in Clearwater, creating positive interactions with the community:

Friendly Greetings: Clearwater residents are known for their friendly demeanor. A warm smile and a simple "hello" go a long way in initiating friendly encounters.

Casual Attire: The overall atmosphere in Clearwater is casual, especially in beachfront areas. Comfortable clothing, including shorts and flip-flops, is widely accepted in many settings.

Respect for Wildlife: Given the coastal environment, respect for wildlife is essential. Avoid feeding or approaching wild animals, including seagulls and dolphins, to maintain their natural behaviors.

Tipping Culture: Tipping is customary in restaurants, and it's common to leave a tip of 15% to 20% for good service. Additionally, tipping may be expected for other services, such as hotel staff and tour guides.

Beach Etiquette: When enjoying the beaches, be mindful of others. Keep noise levels reasonable, and follow any posted rules regarding beach activities.

Cultural Sensitivity: While Clearwater is diverse, being mindful of cultural sensitivity is important. Avoid making assumptions about cultural backgrounds, and be open to learning about the diverse communities in the area.

Language Guide in Clearwater

English is the primary language spoken in Clearwater, and most residents are fluent in it. However, understanding a few local phrases and expressions can enhance your communication:

"Gulfside" or "Beachside": Refers to locations on or near the Gulf of Mexico, often used to describe accommodations, restaurants, or attractions.

"Snowbird": A term used to describe seasonal visitors, often retirees, who migrate to Florida during the winter months to escape colder climates.

"Intercoastal Waterway": The waterway that runs parallel to the Gulf of Mexico, separating

barrier islands from the mainland. It's a significant geographical reference in the area.

"The Intracoastal": Another common term for the Intercoastal Waterway.

"Downtown Clearwater": Refers to the central business district of Clearwater, where you'll find shops, restaurants, and cultural attractions.

"Pinellas County": This is the county where Clearwater is located. Useful when discussing broader geographical areas or directions.

"Clearwater Beach Sunset Festival": Mention this if you're looking for the nightly celebration at Pier 60, where locals and visitors gather to enjoy street performers, vendors, and the breathtaking sunset.

"Sand Key": An island just south of Clearwater Beach, known for its residential areas and quieter atmosphere.

"Causeway": A term for bridges connecting Clearwater to barrier islands, such as the Clearwater Memorial Causeway leading to Clearwater Beach.

"Honeymoon Island": A nearby state park with pristine beaches, ideal for nature walks and bird watching.

"PSTA": The Pinellas Suncoast Transit Authority, which operates buses in the area. This helps when your plan is to use public transportation.

"Dunedin": A neighboring city known for its artsy downtown, Scottish heritage, and vibrant events. Pronounced "duh-NEE-din."

"Tarpon Springs": A city north of Clearwater famous for its Greek heritage, sponge docks, and delicious Greek cuisine.

"Suncoast": A term often used to refer to the coastal region of Florida, encompassing Clearwater and neighboring areas.

"Dolphin Tale": Reference to the famous movie filmed at the Clearwater Marine Aquarium, home to Winter the Dolphin. Useful when discussing local attractions.

"Sand Castle Capital of the World": A playful title often associated with Clearwater Beach, known for its annual sand sculpting competitions.

Using these phrases can enhance your interactions with locals and show your appreciation for the unique aspects of Clearwater's culture and geography. Whether you're seeking directions or engaging in casual conversations, incorporating these local expressions adds a friendly and authentic touch to your travel experience.

Communication and Connectivity in Clearwater

Staying connected and understanding communication options is essential for a seamless experience in Clearwater:

Mobile Networks: Clearwater has reliable mobile network coverage, and major carriers provide good service in the area. Check with your provider regarding international roaming if needed.

Wi-Fi Availability: Most hotels, restaurants, and public spaces offer Wi-Fi. Confirm the availability of Wi-Fi when booking accommodations, and inquire about any associated fees.

Emergency Services: In case of emergencies, dial 911 for immediate assistance. Clearwater has well-established emergency services to ensure the safety of residents and visitors.

Public Transportation Information: Stay informed about public transportation options. PSTA (Pinellas Suncoast Transit Authority) operates buses in the area, providing a convenient way to explore beyond walking distance.

Local Information Centers: Visit local information centers for maps, brochures, and assistance. The Clearwater Regional Chamber of Commerce is a valuable resource for visitors seeking information about the city.

International Visitors: If you're an international visitor, consider obtaining a SIM card for local calls and data usage. Additionally, check if your accommodation provides international calling services.

Social Media: Follow local businesses, attractions, and tourism boards on social media platforms for real-time updates, special promotions, and insights into local events.

By understanding local customs, embracing the language nuances, and staying connected, you'll seamlessly integrate into the vibrant community of Clearwater, ensuring a more immersive and enjoyable travel experience.

CONCLUSION

Final Tips for Travel in Clearwater

As you wrap up your Clearwater adventure, consider these final tips for a memorable and stress-free experience:

Weather Preparedness: Take note of the weather conditions upon your visit. Pack sunscreen, a hat, and light clothing for the sunny days, and have a light jacket for cooler evenings.

Hydration is Key: Florida's climate can be warm and humid. Stay hydrated by carrying a reusable water bottle and drinking plenty of fluids, especially if you're engaging in outdoor activities.

Time Your Visits: Popular attractions may be less crowded during weekdays or in the off-peak season. Plan your visits accordingly for a more relaxed experience.

Local Events: Check local event calendars for festivals, concerts, and special events happening during your stay. Attending local events adds an extra layer of cultural enrichment to your trip.

Sunset Rituals: Join the Sunset at Pier 60 Festival or find a beachside spot to witness the spectacular Gulf Coast sunsets. It's a cherished local tradition.

Explore Beyond Clearwater: Consider exploring nearby areas like Dunedin, Tarpon Springs, and St. Petersburg for diverse experiences, each with its own unique charm.

Photography Opportunities: Capture the beauty of Clearwater with your camera or smartphone. From stunning beaches to vibrant sunsets, there are plenty of picturesque moments to seize.

Respect the Environment: Practice responsible tourism by respecting natural habitats, avoiding littering, and following Leave No Trace principles. This ensures the preservation of Clearwater's natural beauty for future generations.

Sustainable Travel Practices in Clearwater

Clearwater, with its ecological treasures, encourages sustainable travel practices. Here's how you can minimize your environmental impact during your visit:

Choose Eco-Friendly Accommodations: Look for accommodations that prioritize sustainability initiatives, such as energy-efficient practices, waste reduction, and water conservation.

Opt for Public Transportation: Consider using public transportation, like PSTA buses, to explore Clearwater and nearby areas. It's an eco-friendly way to travel and reduces traffic congestion.

Reusable Items: Bring reusable items like water bottles, shopping bags, and utensils to minimize single-use plastic waste. Many businesses in Clearwater support sustainability efforts.

Support Local and Sustainable Dining: Choose restaurants that emphasize locally sourced ingredients and sustainable practices. This not only supports local businesses but also reduces the carbon footprint of your meals.

Respect Wildlife: When enjoying outdoor activities, maintain a safe distance from wildlife, and avoid disturbing their habitats. Follow guidelines for responsible wildlife viewing.

Conserve Water: Be mindful of water usage, especially during dry seasons. Turn off faucets when not in use, and consider reusing towels to reduce laundry frequency in hotels.

Participate in Community Cleanups: Check for local beach cleanup events or community initiatives during your stay. Joining these efforts contributes to the preservation of Clearwater's pristine environment.

Leaving Feedback for a Fulfilling Travel Experience

Sharing your feedback is valuable for both fellow travelers and the local community. Here's how to leave constructive feedback:

Online Reviews: Consider leaving reviews on platforms like TripAdvisor, Yelp, or Google Reviews. Highlight positive experiences and provide constructive feedback for areas that could be improved.

Hotel Surveys: If your accommodation sends a post-stay survey, take the time to fill it out. Your insights can assist the hotel in enhancing its services for future guests.

Social Media: Share your experiences on social media platforms, using relevant hashtags and tagging businesses. This not only provides feedback but also allows others to discover hidden gems based on your recommendations.

Direct Communication: If you had a particularly positive or challenging experience, consider reaching out directly to the establishment. Many businesses appreciate direct communication and use customer feedback for continuous improvement.

Be Specific: When leaving feedback, be specific about your experiences. Mention particular staff members, dishes, or services that stood out. This specificity adds credibility to your feedback.

Constructive Criticism: If you encountered challenges during your trip, frame your feedback as constructive criticism. Highlight areas where improvement is needed and suggest potential solutions.

By sharing your experiences and insights, you contribute to the collective knowledge of the travel community and assist local businesses in providing exceptional experiences to future visitors in Clearwater.

In conclusion, Clearwater beckons with its sun-kissed beaches, rich cultural tapestry, and vibrant community spirit. Whether you're strolling along the iconic Pier 60, savoring a grouper sandwich, or immersing yourself in the local arts scene, Clearwater offers a diverse array of experiences. As you explore this coastal paradise, remember to embrace the friendly local customs, practice sustainable travel, and leave behind feedback to enrich the journeys of those who follow. From the crystal-clear waters to the vibrant cultural scene, Clearwater invites you to create lasting memories along Florida's Gulf Coast. Safe travels!

APPENDIX

Index

Alphabetical list of Topics and Locations Cover in the Guide

Topics

Accommodation Options

Clearwater Beach

Clearwater Brief History

Clearwater Geography and Climate

Communication and Connectivity

Cultural Experience

Locations Covered

Frenchy's Clearwater Beach Restaurants

Kiku Japanese Restaurant

Marina Cantina

Palm Pavilion Beachside Grill & Bar

Pier 60

Pinellas County

Safety Harbor Art and Music Center

St. Petersburg

Tampa

Tarpon Springs

The Intracoastal

Ybor City

SAFE JOURNEY AND HAPPY TRAVELING